Chinese

Inventive and healthy cooking,
for every day and special occasions

© 1998 Rebo International b.v.,The Netherlands
1998 Published by Rebo Productions Ltd., London
Designed and created by Consortium, England

Recipes and photographs © Quadrillion Publishing Ltd,
Godalming, Surrey GU7 1XW
Production co-ordination: Daphne Wannee
Typeset by MATS, Southend-on-Sea, Essex
Printed in Slovenia
Illustrations by Camilla Sopwith
ISBN 1 84053 039 1
J0242 UK

Chinese

Inventive and healthy cooking, for every day and special occasions

REBO
PRODUCTIONS

Contents

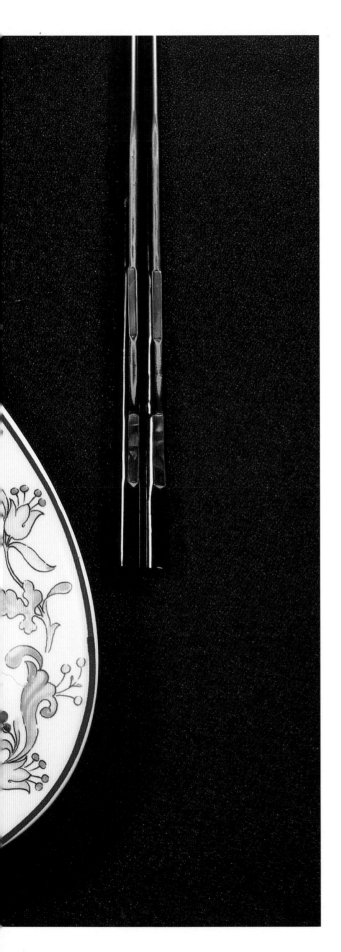

Introduction

Chinese cooking is one of the greatest cuisines in the world – and one of the most popular outside of its homeland. Ancient as it is in origin, Chinese cuisine has a strong appeal to contemporary tastes and lifestyles. It is full of variety and invention; light, healthy and low in fat; attractive to the eye and often quick and easy to execute.

Stir-frying is a common feature throughout the various regional cooking styles of China. Using a wok – an essential item in Chinese cookery – ingredients can be cooked very quickly in a minimum amount of oil. This technique ensures that each ingredient in a dish is cooked and yet retains its individual taste, goodness and texture.

Chinese cooking uses a variety of what we would regard as specialist ingredients, such as dried black mushrooms, lotus roots, Chinese noodles, Shaoxing rice wine, etc. These ingredients are now widely available even from supermarkets, and certainly from the many specialist suppliers and shops nationwide. Stock up on these Chinese storecupboard staples so that you have all you need in hand when you choose to cook a Chinese meal or dish.

This books presents a range of different Chinese-style dishes which draw on the rich variety of culinary styles of the authentic cuisine. Some are highly seasoned and chilli hot; others are characterised by a subtle blend of flavours. There are quick-to-prepare light dishes full of colour and texture, and other much richer, more elaborate dishes. If you are planning a special occasion meal, try some of the truly exotic dishes on offer, featuring luxury ingredients. For more 'everyday' cooking, there is a wide range of exciting and inviting dishes to prepare, whether it's a fragrant soup for a light lunch, a succulent chicken or pork dish for a main course, a crisp and colourful salad for a starter or a medley of Chinese stir-fried vegetables for a side dish. To round off your meal in a perfect way, there are desserts full of luscious fruits – a treat for the eye and the tastebuds.

Imperial Pork Rolls

These fried rice paper rolls are filled with a mixture of bean sprouts, black mushrooms and pork, and are served with a spicy fish sauce.

Preparation time: 40 minutes, plus 15 minutes soaking time • Cooking time: 15 minutes • Serves: 4

Ingredients

2.5 ml (½ tsp) vinegar	300 g (10½ oz) boned pork shoulder, very finely chopped
15 ml (1 tbsp) water	2.5 ml (½ tsp) cornflour
15 ml (1 tbsp) fish sauce	2.5 ml (½ tsp) oil
5 ml (1 tsp) sugar	100 g (3½ oz) bean sprouts, blanched and drained
2.5 ml (½ tsp) finely chopped root ginger	15 ml (1 tbsp) soy sauce
A few drops of chilli sauce	Salt and freshly ground black pepper
4 dried Chinese black mushrooms, soaked for 15 minutes in warm water and drained	16 sheets rice paper, soaked in warm water for 10 minutes
	A little beaten egg
	100 ml (3½ fl oz) oil

Method

1

To make the sauce, in a small serving bowl, mix together the vinegar, water, fish sauce, sugar and ginger and allow to stand for 30 minutes. Add the chilli sauce just before serving.

2

Meanwhile, chop the mushrooms very finely. Toss the pork in the cornflour.

3

Heat the 2.5 ml (½ tsp) oil in a wok and stir-fry the pork, bean sprouts and soy sauce for 2 minutes. Allow to cool. The mixture should be quite dry. Add salt, pepper and chilli sauce to taste.

4

Drain the rice paper sheets and spread them out onto a clean work surface. Place a little of the cooled filling in the centre of each sheet, roll up and seal the edges with a little beaten egg.

5

Heat the 100 ml (3½ fl oz) of oil in a wok and fry the rolls gently on all sides, beginning with the sealed side, until golden brown. Drain on absorbent kitchen paper.

6

Serve the rolls hot with the accompanying sauce.

Serving suggestion

Serve the rolls with lettuce leaves and fresh mint. Guests should wrap the mint and lettuce leaves around the rolls before dipping into the sauce.

Variation

Use fresh Shiitake or oyster mushrooms in place of the dried and soaked Chinese black mushrooms.

Crab Rolls

Chinese pancakes are first filled with a delicious crab mixture, then rolled up and quick-fried until crisp and golden.

Preparation time: 25 minutes • Cooking time: 30 minutes • Serves: 4

Ingredients

For the batter	For the filling
75 g (2¾ oz) plain flour, sieved	450 g (1 lb) cooked crab meat
Salt	2 eggs, beaten
4 eggs, beaten	15 ml (1 tbsp) chopped spring onion
100 ml (3½ fl oz) water	15 ml (1 tbsp) chopped fresh chives
	Salt and freshly ground black pepper, to taste
	5 ml (1 tsp) soy sauce
	50 ml (2 fl oz) oil

Method

1

To make the batter, in a large bowl, mix together the flour, salt, eggs and water. Beat the mixture well and set aside to rest for 10 minutes.

2

Meanwhile, to make the filling, in a separate bowl, mix together the crab meat, 1 beaten egg, spring onion, chives, salt and pepper and soy sauce.

3

Heat 15 ml (1 tbsp) of the oil in a wok and stir-fry the filling mixture for 20 seconds.
Remove from the wok and set aside to cool.

4

Use the batter to make pancakes. Cook them one at a time in a frying pan, using as little oil as necessary, until lightly browned on each side. Keep the cooked pancakes covered and warm while cooking the remainder.

5

Place a little of the cooked filling mixture in the centre of each pancake. Fold up the bottom of each pancake, then fold over the side flaps. Roll up each pancake, beginning at the bottom where the filling is visible. Brush the edges lightly with the remaining beaten egg to seal. Set the rolls aside for a few minutes.

6

Heat the remaining oil in a frying pan and fry the rolls gently on each side until crisp and golden brown. Remove from the oil, drain on absorbent kitchen paper and serve immediately.

Serving suggestion

Make a delicious sauce to accompany these rolls by mixing together 15 ml (1 tbsp) fish sauce, 100 ml (3½ fl oz) fish stock, 10 ml (2 tsp) sugar and 5 ml (1 tsp) chopped root ginger.

Variation

Use finely chopped cooked shelled prawns in place of the crab meat.

Cook's tip

Cook the pancakes in a non-stick frying pan to avoid using oil.

Chinese Ravioli

Steamed Chinese ravioli with a satisfying filling of pork and Chinese leaves.

Preparation time: 20 minutes • Cooking time: 25 minutes • Serves: 4

Ingredients

450 g (1 lb) pork, finely diced	Salt and freshly ground pepper
225 g (8 oz) Chinese leaves, finely sliced	16 wonton wrappers (Chinese ravioli)
1 spring onion, chopped	1 egg, beaten
15 ml (1 tbsp) soy sauce	5 ml (1 tsp) sesame oil

Method

1

In a bowl, mix together the pork, Chinese leaves, spring onion and soy sauce. Season with salt and pepper. Leave to marinate for 30 minutes, stirring occasionally.

2

Peel off the wonton wrappers one by one and place a little of the drained filling on each. Keep the filling away from the edges of the wrappers. Brush the edges of the wrappers with beaten egg.

3

Fold the wrappers in half, pushing the filling into the centre and pushing out any trapped air. Seal the edges well with your fingers, then cut off any excess dough with a knife or pastry cutter.

4

Place a clean damp tea towel in the base of a Chinese bamboo steamer. Place the ravioli directly onto the tea towel and cover. Place the steamer over a wok or large pan of boiling water and steam the ravioli for about 15 minutes. Turn over once halfway through cooking and brush with sesame oil.

5

If you have any filling left over, heat a little oil in a wok and stir-fry the filling for about 1 minute. Serve with the ravioli.

Serving suggestion

Serve with a dipping sauce (see page 14 for recipe).

Variation

Use finely diced beef in place of the pork.

Cook's tips

It is important to seal the edges of the ravioli firmly before steaming, otherwise the filling will leak out. Any excess dough trimmed off in Step 3 can be cut into small pieces and added to a soup.

Spring Rolls

Stuffed spring rolls, served slightly chilled, make a wonderful pre-dinner appetiser.

Preparation time: 30 minutes, plus 15 minutes soaking time • Cooking time: 10 minutes • Serves: 4

Ingredients

1 large cooked pork chop	*18 square sheets rice paper, soaked for 10 minutes in water*
100 g (3½ oz) cooked chicken	
5 ml (1 tsp) soy sauce	**For the sauce**
5 ml (1 tsp) sugar	*30 ml (2 tbsp) water*
30 ml (2 tbsp) sesame oil	*Juice of ½ lemon*
50g (1¾ oz) bamboo shoots, blanched	*5 ml (1 tsp) sugar*
225 g (8 oz) bean sprouts	*1 clove garlic, chopped*
1 Chinese mushroom, soaked for 15 minutes in warm water, drained and thinly sliced	*30 ml (2 tbsp) carrot, cut into thin strips*
	30 ml (2 tbsp) courgette, cut into thin strips
5 ml (1 tsp) cornflour, combined with a little water	*30 ml (2 tbsp) fish sauce*

Method

1
Remove the pork meat from the bone and cut into thin strips. Cut the chicken into thin strips.

2
In a bowl, mix together the meats with the soy sauce, sugar and 15 ml (1 tbsp) sesame oil. Allow to marinate until required.

3
Heat the remaining sesame oil in a wok and stir-fry the bamboo shoots, bean sprouts
and mushroom for about 2-3 minutes, until tender.

4
Add the meat mixture and the marinade to the wok. Stir well and heat through.

5
Stir in the cornflour paste and cook until the sauce has thickened. Set the wok aside and
allow the contents to cool completely.

6
Drain the rice paper sheets. Place a little filling on each of the sheets. Fold up the bottom half of each sheet, then fold over the
side flaps. Fold up each sheet, beginning at the bottom where the filling is visible, and brush the edges lightly with water to seal.
Allow the rolls to dry. Chill in the refrigerator.

7
Meanwhile, to make the sauce, mix together all the ingredients in a small serving bowl.

8
Serve the rolls with the sauce separately.

Serving suggestion
Serve the rolls on a bed of shredded crisp lettuce.

Variation
Use cooked turkey or duck in place of the chicken.

Cook's tip
For the best results, if time permits, stir-fry the bean sprouts, mushroom and bamboo shoots separately,
then mix together just before placing the filling on the rice paper.

Crab Soup with Ginger

This deliciously flavoured soup, with fresh crab and a hint of ginger, is perfect for serving as part of a special dinner.

Preparation time: 40 minutes, plus about 35 minutes cooling time • Cooking time: 50 minutes • Serves: 4

Ingredients

1 carrot, chopped	700 ml (1¼ pints) fish stock
1 onion, chopped	2.5-cm (1-inch) piece root ginger, chopped
½ leek, chopped	
1 bay leaf	15 ml (1 tsp) sake
2 medium-sized uncooked crabs	Salt and freshly ground pepper

Method

1
Place the carrot, onion, leek and bay leaf in a large saucepan and add 1 litre (1¾ pints) water. Bring to the boil and add the crabs. Allow to bowl briskly for 20 minutes, or until the crabs are cooked.

2
Remove the crabs and allow to cool. Once cooled, break off the pincers and break the joints, cut open the back and open the claws. Carefully remove all the crab meat.

3
Bring the stock to the boil and add the ginger, sake and crab meat. Boil for 15 minutes.

4
Check the seasoning, adding salt and pepper as necessary. Serve very hot.

Serving suggestion
Serve in individual bowls garnished with fresh herb sprigs.

Variation
If sake is not available, use dry sherry instead.

Cook's tip
Prepare the soup the day before. If allowed to rest overnight, the flavours of the soup will develop. Reheat gently just before serving.

Turkey Soup with Black Mushrooms

An unusual blend of ingredients and flavours which makes a tasty, warming soup.

Preparation time: 8 minutes, plus 15 minutes soaking time • Cooking time: 35 minutes • Serves: 4

Ingredients

150 g (5½ oz) turkey breast	*700 ml (1¼ pints) chicken stock*
15 ml (1 tbsp) sesame oil	*15 ml (1 tbsp) soy sauce*
50 g (1¾ oz) dried black Chinese mushrooms, soaked for 15 minutes in warm water and drained	*1 slice root ginger*
	Salt and freshly ground black pepper, to taste

Method

1

Cut the turkey breast into slices, then into small cubes.

2

Heat the oil in a wok and stir-fry the turkey until brown. Remove from the pan and drain off all the excess oil.

3

Cook the mushrooms in boiling, salted water for 10 minutes. Rinse and drain well.

4

Place the mushrooms in a saucepan with the stock. Stir in the turkey, soy sauce, ginger and salt and pepper.

5

Bring to the boil, then simmer gently for 15 minutes.

6

Remove the slice of ginger before serving the soup piping hot.

Serving suggestion

Serve in individual bowls and sprinkle with chopped fresh chives.

Variation

Use chicken breast in place of the turkey.

Chicken and Sweetcorn Soup

This hearty, slightly spicy soup combines baby corn cobs and cooked chicken.

Preparation time: 15 minutes • Cooking time: 30 minutes • Serves: 4

Ingredients

150 g (5½ oz) canned sweetcorn	*2.5-cm (1-inch) piece root ginger, chopped*
700 ml (1¼ pints) chicken stock	*30 ml (2 tbsp) light soy sauce*
2 medium-sized cooked chicken breasts	*A few drops of chilli sauce*
12 baby corn cobs	*Salt and freshly ground pepper, to taste*

Method

1

Place the canned sweetcorn in a food processor with 100 ml (3½ fl oz) of the stock. Process until smooth.

2

Strain the sweetcorn purée through a sieve, using the back of a large spoon to push it through.

3

Cut the chicken into thin slices. Place the remaining stock in a saucepan and stir in the chicken slices.

4

Add the sweetcorn purée and the baby corn, and stir. Cover, bring to the boil and simmer for 15 minutes. Add the ginger and soy sauce, and continue cooking for a further 10 minutes.

5

Add the chilli sauce and stir. Check the seasoning and add salt and pepper if necessary. Serve.

Serving suggestion

Serve this quick and easy soup as a substantial starter to any Chinese meal.

Variation

Use creamed sweetcorn in place of the puréed canned sweetcorn.

Cook's tip

Use home-made chicken stock for the best flavour.

Peking-Style Soup

Duck stock is the base of this filling soup, which is flavoured with sesame seeds and soy sauce.

Preparation time: 15 minutes • Cooking time: 25 minutes • Serves: 4

Ingredients

4 slices smoked ham	15 ml (1 tbsp) soy sauce
700 ml (1¼ pints) duck stock	2.5 ml (½ tsp) white wine vinegar
300 g (10½ oz) Chinese leaves	Salt and freshly ground black pepper, to taste
15 ml (1 tbsp) sesame seeds	
A pinch of chopped garlic	1 egg yolk, beaten

Method

1
Cut the ham into small, evenly sized cubes.

2
Place the duck stock in a saucepan and heat until simmering. Cut the Chinese leaves into small pieces and add to the stock. Simmer for 10 minutes.

3
Stir in the sesame seeds, garlic, ham, soy sauce, vinegar and salt and pepper.

4
Cook for 10 minutes over gentle heat. Using a teaspoon, carefully drizzle the beaten egg yolk into the soup. Serve immediately.

Serving suggestion
Garnish with chopped fresh herbs before serving.

Variation
Use smoked beef, chicken or duck in place of the smoked ham.

Bamboo Shoot Soup

Beaten egg sieved into the hot soup gives this dish strong visual appeal.

Preparation time: 10 minutes, plus 15 minutes soaking time • Cooking time: 45 minutes • Serves: 4

Ingredients

100 g (3½ oz) bamboo shoots, cut into thin matchsticks	30 ml (2 tbsp) light soy sauce
4 dried Chinese black mushrooms, soaked for 15 minutes in warm water and drained	Salt and freshly ground black pepper, to taste
	2.5 ml (½ tsp) cornflour, combined with a little water
700 ml (1¼ pints) chicken stock	1 egg
15 ml (1 tbsp) wine vinegar	10 fresh chives

Method

1

Blanch the bamboo shoots in boiling, salted water for 3 minutes. Rinse and set aside to drain.

2

Cook the mushrooms in boiling, salted water for 10 minutes. Rinse and set aside to drain.

3

Bring the stock to the boil and add the bamboo shoots, mushrooms, vinegar and soy sauce. Season with salt and pepper. Simmer for 10 minutes.

4

Stir in the cornflour paste and bring the soup slowly back to the boil.

5

Reduce the heat. Beat the egg thoroughly. Place the beaten egg in a sieve and add to the soup by shaking the sieve back and forth over the pan.

6

Add the chives and serve the soup piping hot.

Serving suggestion

Garnish the soup with sprigs of fresh flat-leafed parsley before serving.

Cook's tip

Make sure the soup is boiling hot before adding the beaten egg.

Fish and Rice Soup

This fish soup is delicately flavoured with fresh root ginger.

Preparation time: 10 minutes • Cooking time: 25-30 minutes • Serves: 4

Ingredients

700 ml (1¼ pints) fish stock	2.5 ml (½ tsp) cornflour, combined with a little water
15 ml (1 tbsp) soy sauce	300 g (10½ oz) fresh cod or haddock fillet
1 slice root ginger, chopped	100 g (3½ oz) long-grain rice, part-cooked (see 'Cook's tip')
300 g (12 oz) fresh cod or haddock fillet	Salt and freshly ground pepper, to taste

Method

1

In a large saucepan, gently heat the stock, soy sauce and ginger. Stir in the cornflour paste and simmer gently for 10 minutes.

2

Meanwhile, cut the fish fillet into very thin slices, then into strips. Set aside.

3

Stir the rice into the soup and simmer for 5 minutes. Remove from the heat and add the fish.

4

Allow the fish to cook in the hot soup for 5-10 minutes. Check the seasoning, adding salt and pepper as necessary, and serve immediately.

Serving suggestion

Garnish with fresh herb sprigs or chopped fresh herbs before serving.

Variation

Any variety of fish can be used in this recipe, but remember to slice it very thinly.

Cook's tip

It is best to use rice that has been cooked in boiling, salted water for about 3 minutes.

Abalone Soup

Canned abalone cooked in fish stock and flavoured with oyster and soy sauces – absolutely delicious!

Preparation time: 10 minutes • Cooking time: 25 minutes • Serves: 4

Ingredients

700 ml (1¼ pints) fish stock	*15 ml (1 tbsp) soy sauce*
6 canned abalone, plus 30 ml (2 tbsp) reserved juice from the can	*10 ml (2 tsp) oyster sauce*
	1 egg white
½ spring onion, chopped	*Salt and freshly ground black pepper, to taste*

Method

1

In a saucepan, gently heat the stock, reserved abalone juice, spring onion and soy and oyster sauces.

2

Cut the canned abalone into thin slices, then into matchsticks. Add to the stock and simmer gently for 15 minutes.

3

Beat the egg white lightly. Heat the soup until boiling, then gradually stir in the egg white.

4

Season with salt and pepper and serve immediately.

Serving suggestion

Garnish with chopped fresh chives and a sprig of fresh parsley before serving.

Variation

Use chicken stock in place of the fish stock.

Cook's tip

Lightly beat the egg white and add slowly to the boiling soup, so that it thickens immediately.

Scrambled Eggs with Crab Meat

The flavour of fresh crab meat combines beautifully with creamy scrambled eggs.

Preparation time: 40 minutes, plus 15 minutes soaking time and about 35 minutes cooling time •
Cooking time: 40 minutes • Serves: 4

Ingredients

3 dried Chinese black mushrooms, soaked for 15 minutes in warm water and drained	8 eggs, beaten
1 carrot, chopped	A few drops of sesame oil
1 leek, chopped	5 ml (1 tsp) sake
1 onion, chopped	15 ml (1 tbsp) soy sauce
1 large uncooked crab	Salt and freshly ground black pepper, to taste

Method

1
Cook the mushrooms in boiling, salted water for 15 minutes. Rinse in fresh water, set aside to drain, then thinly slice.

2
Place the carrot, leek and onion in a large saucepan. Add 2 litres (3½ pints) water and bring to the boil.
Add the crab and cook for 15 minutes. Remove the crab and set aside to cool.

3
When the crab is cool enough to handle, break off the pincers, break open the back and all the joints and remove the meat.

4
In a large bowl, mix together the eggs, mushrooms, sesame oil, sake, soy sauce and the crab meat. Season with salt and pepper.

5
In a frying pan, cook the eggs over gentle heat, stirring continuously. When the eggs are cooked
to your liking, serve immediately.

Serving suggestion
Form the scrambled eggs into a round in the centre of individual serving plates. Scatter fine slivers of presoaked
boiled and stir-fried dried Chinese black mushrooms around the eggs and garnish with chopped fresh chives. Add a sprig
of fresh parsley to the centre of the eggs.

Variation
Use ready-cooked crab meat or tinned crab meat for a quick and easy alternative.

Cook's tip
Be careful not to cook the eggs too quickly, or they will become hard and dry.

Whiting Fritters with Cold Fish Sauce

Delicate fillets of whiting in a crisp batter coating, served with a fragrant dipping sauce.

Preparation time: 30 minutes • Cooking time: 20 minutes • Serves: 4

Ingredients

150 g (5½ oz) plain flour, sieved	Oil for deep-frying
5 ml (1 tsp) baking powder	
100 ml (3½ fl oz) water	**For the sauce**
1 egg, beaten	15 ml (1 tbsp) fish sauce
5 ml (1 tsp) oil	15 ml (1 tbsp) soy sauce
Salt	15 ml (1 tbsp) fish stock
450 g (1 lb) whiting fillets	A few fresh mint leaves, finely chopped
Freshly ground black pepper	

Method

1

To make the batter, place the flour and baking powder in a mixing bowl. Gradually mix in the water, then the beaten egg.

2

Add the oil and a good pinch of salt, and beat all the ingredients together well. Set the batter aside to rest for a few minutes.

3

Meanwhile, to make the sauce, mix together all the ingredients in a small serving dish. Set aside.

4

Season the fish fillets with salt and pepper, then cut into small strips.

5

Heat the oil in a deep pan or deep-fryer. In batches, dip the fish strips into the batter and add to the hot oil.
Deep-fry until crisp and golden.

6

Remove the fritters and drain on absorbent kitchen paper. Keep hot while deep-frying the remaining fish strips.

7

Serve the fritters with the fish sauce.

Serving suggestion
Serve the fritters garnished with sprigs of fresh mint.

Variation
If you do not have the sauce ingredients available, the fritters are delicious served with wedges of lemon to squeeze over.

Cook's tip
Make the sauce a few hours before serving, to allow the flavour of the mint to develop.

Prawns with Onions

Diced onions are first marinated, then stir-fried with prawns and served in a soy-flavoured sauce.

Preparation time: 15 minutes, plus 15 minutes marinating time • Cooking time: 20 minutes • Serves: 4

Ingredients

2 large onions, diced	*16 raw prawns, shelled and deveined*
30 ml (2 tbsp) soy sauce	*Salt and freshly ground black pepper, to taste*
10 ml (2 tsp) sugar	
30 ml (2 tbsp) oil	*100 ml (3½ fl oz) fish stock*

Method

1

In a bowl, combine the onions, soy sauce and sugar. Marinate for 15 minutes, stirring frequently.

2

Heat the oil in a wok and stir-fry the prawns for about 5 minutes, until cooked. Remove and keep warm.

3

Add the onions and marinade to the wok and stir-fry gently for 5 minutes. Season with salt and pepper.

4

Add the stock to the wok and continue cooking for a few minutes, until the liquid has considerably reduced. Serve the onions topped with the prawns.

Serving suggestion
Garnish with fresh herb sprigs.

Variation
Replace 2.5-5 ml (½-1 tsp) of the soy sauce with chilli sauce, for a chilli hot alternative.

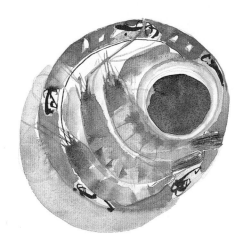

Chinese Leaves with Oysters

Chinese leaves are cooked in fish stock with oysters and bacon – a wonderful flavour combination.

Preparation time: 25 minutes • Cooking time: 10 minutes • Serves: 4

Ingredients

12 large raw oysters in their shells	*225 g (8 oz) unsmoked bacon, diced*
450 g (1 lb) Chinese leaves	*60 ml (4 tbsp) fish stock*
15 ml (1 tbsp) oil	*Salt and freshly ground black pepper*

Method

1
Using a tea towel to hold each oyster, carefully prise open the shells with a sharp-pointed knife. Cut the oysters away from the shells, reserving the meat and juice. Discard the shells.

2
Shred the Chinese leaves.

3
Heat the oil in a wok and stir-fry the bacon for 1 minute, until browned.

4
Stir the Chinese leaves into the wok and add the stock. Check the seasoning, adding salt and pepper to taste. Stir-fry the Chinese leaves until they are cooked to your liking.

5
Place the oysters and their juice on top of the Chinese leaves and poach for 2 minutes.

6
Remove the oysters and place on a hot serving plate with the Chinese leaves. Serve immediately.

Variation
Use smoked bacon or ham in place of the unsmoked bacon.

Cook's tip
If you prefer your oysters well-cooked, increase the cooking time by another 2 minutes. Do not overcook, or they will become chewy.

Prawns with Vegetables

Quick-fried prawns served with a medley of stir-fried Chinese vegetables.

Preparation time: 20 minutes, plus 15 minutes soaking time • Cooking time: 25 minutes • Serves: 4

Ingredients

8 dried Chinese black mushrooms, soaked in warm water for 15 minutes and drained	5 ml (1 tsp) wine vinegar
225 g (8 oz) bean sprouts	Salt and freshly ground black pepper, to taste
½ cucumber	5 ml (1 tsp) oil
30 ml (2 tbsp) peanut oil	20 raw prawns, shelled and deveined
1 clove garlic, chopped	30 ml (2 tbsp) cornflour
5 ml (1 tsp) sugar	15 ml (1 tbsp) soy sauce
5 ml (1 tsp) oyster sauce	15 ml (1 tbsp) sesame oil

Method

1

Cook the mushrooms in boiling, salted water for 15 minutes. Rinse and set aside to drain.

2

Meanwhile, rinse and drain the beans sprouts. Peel the cucumber with a sharp knife and slice into julienne strips.

3

Heat the peanut oil in a wok and stir-fry the garlic, bean sprouts and mushrooms for 1 minute.

4

Add the cucumber, sugar, oyster sauce, wine vinegar and salt and pepper and cook for 2 minutes, stirring continuously.

5

Heat the oil in a frying pan. Toss the prawns in the cornflour and fry for about 5 minutes, until cooked through.

6

Transfer the vegetables to a serving platter. Top with the fried prawns. Sprinkle with soy sauce and sesame oil just before serving.

Serving suggestion

Pile a serving of the vegetables in the centre of each individual serving plate. Position the prawns at intervals around the vegetables, to create a spoke-like arrangement. Intersperse drops of soy sauce and sesame oil around the prawns and vegetables, to create a decorative effect. Add a sprig of fresh herbs to the centre of the dish.

Cook's tip

To devein prawns, remove the black thread from the indentation along the back of the prawn with a small, sharp knife.

Scallops with Asparagus

Fresh asparagus spears make a wonderful accompaniment for tender scallops, served with a sweet-and-sour dipping sauce.

Preparation time: 35 minutes • Cooking time: 15 minutes • Serves: 4

Ingredients

16 scallops in their shells		*For the dipping sauce*
16 fresh asparagus spears		*15 ml (1 tbsp) soy sauce*
30 ml (2 tbsp) oil		*10 ml (2 tsp) sugar*
Salt and freshly ground black pepper		*½ spring onion, finely chopped*
		15 ml (1 tbsp) oil
		5 ml (1 tsp) wine vinegar
		Salt and freshly ground black pepper, to taste

Method

1

With the point of a sharp knife, prise open the scallops and extract the scallops and corals. Rinse well and allow to dry on absorbent kitchen paper.

2

Boil the asparagus in salt water until tender, then refresh in cold water. Drain and halve lengthwise.

3

Meanwhile, to make the dipping sauce, combine all the ingredients in a small serving dish. Set aside.

4

Brush the scallops and corals with oil, and season with salt and pepper.

5

Preheat the grill. Grill the scallops under a high heat for 1 minute. Turn gently and cook the other side for 1 minute.

6

Serve the scallops and asparagus together to dip in the sauce.

Serving suggestion

Arrange a decorative combination of scallops and asparagus spears on serving plates, interspersed with small pools of sauce for dipping. Garnish with fresh herb sprigs.

Variation

Instead of grilling, the scallops can be quickly but gently fried in oil in a frying pan or wok.

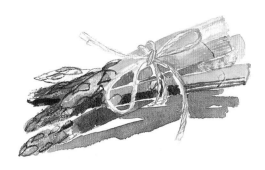

Steamed Prawns

Fresh prawns, eye-catchingly garnished with courgette peel, are steamed and served with a mint-flavoured fish sauce.

Preparation time: 40 minutes • Cooking time: 10 minutes, if done in 2 batches • Serves: 4

Ingredients

15 ml (1 tbsp) fish sauce	*10 fresh mint leaves, finely chopped*
15 ml (1 tbsp) water	*1 shallot, chopped*
15 ml (1 tbsp) wine vinegar	*Salt and freshly ground black pepper, to taste*
15 ml (1 tbsp) soy sauce	*12 raw prawns, shelled and deveined*
5 ml (1 tsp) sugar	*2 medium-sized courgettes*

Method

1

In a small serving bowl, mix together the fish sauce, water, wine vinegar, soy sauce, sugar, mint, shallot
and salt and pepper. Stir well and set aside for at least 1 hour.

2

Meanwhile, peel the courgettes, then cut the peel into 12 long strips.

3

Season the prawns with plenty of salt and pepper. Roll a strip of courgette around each prawn and steam, in 2 batches,
in a Chinese bamboo steamer over a large pan or wok of boiling water for 5 minutes.

4

Serve the prawns hot, accompanied by the sauce.

Variation

Use finely chopped fresh coriander in place of the mint in the sauce.

Cook's tip

If the strips of courgette peel are not very pliable, blanch in boiling water for 30 seconds before wrapping around the prawns.

Stir-Fried Lobster with Ginger

Fresh lobster sautéed with courgettes in a pungent fish sauce.

Preparation time: 45 minutes, plus about 35 minutes cooling time • Cooking time: 25 minutes • Serves: 4

Ingredients

2 lobsters, each weighing 350 g (12 oz)	*10 ml (2 tsp) chopped root ginger*
Salt	*15 ml (1 tbsp) oyster sauce*
15 ml (1 tbsp) vinegar	*100 ml (3½ fl oz) fish stock*
1 courgette	*5 ml (1 tsp) cornflour, combined with a little water*
15 ml (1 tbsp) oil	*Freshly ground black pepper*

Method

1

To cook the lobsters, fill a large saucepan with water and add a little salt and the vinegar. Boil the lobsters for 15 minutes. Drain, allow to cool, then extract the lobster meat.

2

Slice the lobster meat into bite-sized pieces.

3

Slice the courgette into thin matchsticks.

4

In a wok, heat the oil and stir-fry the ginger for a few seconds. Add the courgette and stir-fry for about 30 seconds, until tender but still crisp. Add the lobster and heat through, stirring.

5

Pour in the oyster sauce and stock, season with salt and pepper to taste and allow the liquid to reduce.

6

Add the cornflour paste, stirring continuously, and cook until thickened. Serve immediately.

Serving suggestion
Serve with boiled Chinese egg noodles.

Variation
Use fresh crawfish or crab in place of the lobster.

Cook's tip
Use a nutcracker to break open the lobster claws.

Chicken Breasts with Spring Onion

Stuffed chicken breasts, steamed and served in a light sauce.

Preparation time: 20 minutes • Cooking time: 30 minutes • Serves: 4

Ingredients

1 spring onion, cut into rounds	*175 ml (6 fl oz) chicken stock*
1 carrot, cut into thin julienne strips	*15 ml (1 tbsp) soy sauce*
5 ml (1 tsp) chopped garlic	*2.5 ml (½ tsp) sugar*
4 chicken breasts	*5 ml (1 tsp) cornflour, combined with*
Salt and freshly ground black pepper	*a little water*

Method

1

Mix together the spring onion, carrot and half the garlic.

2

Slice the chicken breasts open lengthwise without cutting through them completely. Open out.

3

Season the insides with salt and pepper and divide the vegetable stuffing between the 4 breasts.

4

Pull the top half of each breast back into place. Season the outsides of the breasts with salt and pepper. Place in a Chinese bamboo steamer and steam over a large pan or wok of boiling water for about 15 minutes, until cooked through.

5

Place the stock in a small saucepan and bring to the boil. Stir in the soy sauce, sugar and the remaining garlic.
Simmer and allow to reduce for a few minutes.

6

Add the cornflour paste to the sauce and stir continuously until thickened.

7

Sliced the stuffed chicken breasts and serve with the sauce spooned over.

Serving suggestion

Serve with plain boiled or steamed rice garnished with 15 ml (1 tbsp) chopped fresh chives.

Cook's tip

Be sure to cut the onion and carrot very thinly so that they cook during the steaming.

Chicken with Bamboo Shoots

Quick-fried chicken and bamboo shoots, served in a tasty ginger and oyster sauce.

Preparation time: 25 minutes • Cooking time: 15 minutes • Serves: 4

Ingredients

225 g (8 oz) whole bamboo shoots or canned, sliced bamboo shoots	2.5 ml (½ tsp) chopped root ginger
15 ml (1 tbsp) sesame oil	15 ml (1 tbsp) Shaoxing rice wine
1 medium-sized chicken, boned and the meat cut into thin slices	15 ml (1 tbsp) oyster sauce
	300 ml (½ pint) chicken stock
5 ml (1 tsp) chopped garlic	Salt and freshly ground black pepper, to taste
	5 ml (1 tsp) cornflour, combined with a little water

Method

1

Cut the bamboo shoots in half lengthwise, then cut into thin, half-moon shaped slices.

2

Blanch the slices of bamboo shoot in boiling water, drain and rinse in cold water. Set aside to drain thoroughly.

3

Meanwhile, heat the sesame oil in a wok and stir-fry the chicken, garlic and ginger for about 2 minutes.

4

Pour off any excess fat. Add the wine to the wok and stir to remove any crisp bits from the pan.

5

Stir in the oyster sauce and stock. Add the bamboo shoots, season with salt and pepper and cook for 2 minutes, stirring.

6

Add the cornflour paste to the wok and stir continuously until the sauce thickens. Serve immediately.

Serving suggestion

Serve with stir-fried mangetout and baby corn cobs.

Variation

Sesame oil lends a strong, distinctive flavour to this dish. As a milder-flavoured alternative,
use half peanut oil and half sesame oil.

Braised Chicken with Ginger

Boned chicken, coated with ginger and cooked in a vegetable and ginger-flavoured stock.

Preparation time: 1 hour • Cooking time: 1 hour • Serves: 4

Ingredients

1 medium-sized chicken, boned	1 turnip, diced
2.5 ml (½ tsp) finely chopped root ginger	1 courgette, diced
Salt and freshly ground pepper	1 onion, thinly sliced
1 carrot, diced	5 slices of root ginger

Method

1

Remove the breast and leg meat from the chicken and set aside. Keep the meat from each leg in one piece.

2

Place the remaining meat, bones and carcass in a large saucepan and just cover with water. Bring to the boil and continue to boil until the liquid has reduced to ¼ of its original quantity. Strain the stock through a fine sieve.

3

Sprinkle the chopped ginger on the inside of the 2 pieces of leg meat and season with salt and pepper.
Roll up each leg tightly and secure with kitchen string.

4

Place the strained stock in a saucepan and add 150 ml (¼ pint) water. Bring to the boil.

5

Add the prepared vegetables, sliced ginger, rolled leg meat and the 2 breasts. Simmer for about 15 minutes, or until the chicken is cooked through.

6

Remove the rolled leg meat, cut off the string and slice the meat into rounds. Arrange the slices on warmed serving plates.

7

Remove the chicken breasts and thinly slice. Arrange the slices on serving plates alongside the leg slices. Using a slotted spoon, remove the vegetables from the stock and arrange around the meat. Pour over a little of the stock and serve immediately.

Serving suggestion

Garnish with whole fresh chives and serve with plain boiled or steamed rice.

Cook's tip

If you are short of time, do not bone the legs but simply cut slits at intervals in the meat. Insert the chopped ginger into the slits.

Chicken in Hot Pepper Sauce

Stir-fried chicken served with peppers in a hot and spicy sauce.

Preparation time: 25 minutes • Cooking time: 10 minutes • Serves: 4

Ingredients

1 medium-sized chicken	*15 ml (1 tbsp) light soy sauce*
30 ml (2 tbsp) oil	*5 ml (1 tsp) sugar*
5 ml (1 tsp) chopped garlic	*300 ml (½ pint) chicken stock*
1 red pepper, seeded and cut into thin strips	*15 ml (1 tbsp) chilli sauce*
1 green pepper, seeded and cut into thin strips	*Salt and freshly ground black pepper, to taste*
5 ml (1 tsp) wine vinegar	

Method

1

Remove all the chicken from the bones and carcass. Cut into thin strips.

2

Heat the oil in a wok and stir-fry the garlic, chicken and the peppers for about 2-3 minutes, until browned.

3

Pour off any excess oil. Add the wine vinegar to the wok and stir to remove any crisp bits from the pan.
Stir in the soy sauce, sugar and stock.

4

Gradually stir in the chilli sauce, tasting after each addition for the desired level of heat. Season with salt and pepper.

5

Cook until the sauce has reduced slightly. Serve piping hot.

Serving suggestion

Serve with plain boiled Chinese egg noodles

Variation

Use 1 seeded and finely chopped fresh green chilli pepper in place of the chilli sauce.

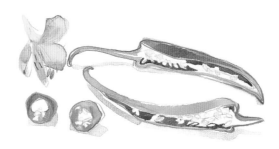

Duckling with Onions

Onions are stir-fried with tender slices of duckling and served in a rich sauce flavoured with Shaoxing rice wine and soy and hoisin sauces.

Preparation time: 20 minutes • Cooking time: 15 minutes • Serves: 4

Ingredients

30 ml (2 tbsp) oil	15 ml (1 tbsp) soy sauce
2 large onions, finely sliced	15 ml (1 tbsp) hoisin sauce
1 duckling, boned and the meat cut into slices	300 ml (½ pint) chicken stock
30 ml (2 tbsp) Shaoxing rice wine	Salt and freshly ground black pepper

Method

1

Heat the oil in a wok and stir-fry the onions until lightly browned. Draw the onions up the side of the wok away from the oil, to keep warm.

2

Add the duckling to the wok and stir-fry until lightly browned.

3

Pour in the wine. Draw the onions back into the bottom of the wok with the duckling.

4

Stir in the soy and hoisin sauces and the stock. Allow the sauce to cook until slightly reduced.

5

Season with salt and pepper and serve immediately.

Serving suggestion

Garnish with fresh flat-leafed parsley sprigs and chopped chives, and serve with Stir-Fried Rice with Peppers (see page 88 for recipe).

Variation

Use duck breast slices if duckling is not available.

Duckling in Five-Spice Sauce

Duckling slices cooked with water chestnuts, Chinese black mushrooms and bamboo shoots and served in a traditional Chinese five-spice sauce.

Preparation time: 20 minutes, plus 15 minutes soaking time • Cooking time: 30 minutes • Serves: 4

Ingredients

12 canned water chestnuts	*4 dried Chinese mushrooms, soaked in warm water for 15 minutes, drained and chopped*
100 g (3½ oz) bamboo shoots	*300 ml (½ pint) duck stock*
15 ml (1 tbsp) sesame oil	*5 ml (1 tsp) five-spice powder*
5 ml (1 tsp) chopped root ginger	*Salt and freshly ground black pepper, to taste*
1 duckling, boned and the meat cut into thin slices	*5 ml (1 tsp) cornflour, combined with a little water*

Method

1
Rinse the water chestnuts and blanch in boiling, lightly salted for 10 minutes. Lift out and set aside to drain.

2
Blanch the bamboo shoots in the same water, rinse and drain. Once well-drained, cut into thin matchsticks.

3
Heat the sesame oil in a wok and stir-fry the ginger and duckling slices for about 2 minutes.

4
Using a slotted spoon, remove the ginger and duckling and set aside. Stir-fry the bamboo shoots, Chinese mushrooms and water chestnuts for about 1 minute.

5
Pour off any excess fat and return the duckling and ginger to the wok. Add the stock and stir well. Sprinkle over the five-spice powder and allow to cook for about 15 minutes.

6
Check the seasoning, adding salt and pepper as necessary. Add the cornflour paste, stirring continuously until the sauce has thickened. Serve immediately.

Serving suggestion
Garnish with fresh herbs and serve with boiled Chinese egg noodles.

Variations
Use chicken stock in place of the duck stock, if not available. Use duck breasts in place of the duckling.

Cook's tip
The water chestnuts will retain their crunchy texture even though cooked through.

Caramelised Spare Ribs

These sweet, caramelised spare ribs are always a success. Tell guests to use their fingers, and provide finger bowls and paper napkins.

Preparation time: 10 minutes • Cooking time: 55 minutes • Serves: 4

Ingredients

1 carrot	15 ml (1 tbsp) white wine vinegar
1 leek	5 ml (1 tsp) chopped garlic
1 bay leaf	30 ml (2 tbsp) soy sauce
900 g (2 lb) pork spare ribs, separated	50 ml (2 fl oz) chicken stock
15 ml (1 tbsp) honey	Salt and freshly ground black pepper

Method

1

Place the carrot, leek and bay leaf in a large saucepan, and add 2 litres (3½ pints) water. Bring to the boil and add the spare ribs. Blanch the meat for 10 minutes, remove from the stock and drain well.

2

Lay the ribs in an ovenproof dish. Combine the honey, wine vinegar and garlic, and spread the mixture all over the ribs.

3

Add the soy sauce and stock to the dish. Season well with salt and pepper.

4

Place in a preheated very hot oven at 240°C/475°F/Gas Mark 9. Cook for about 45 minutes, until the ribs are caramelised and have turned a rich, dark brown colour. Serve immediately.

Serving suggestion

Serve on a bed of finely shredded crisp lettuce lightly seasoned with salt and pepper.

Pork Slices with Crunchy Vegetables

This dish has a cold sauce to accompany the lightly steamed vegetables and thinly sliced pork.

Preparation time: 25 minutes, plus 30 minutes standing time • Cooking time: 10 minutes • Serves: 4

Ingredients

15 ml (1 tbsp) light soy sauce	450 g (1 lb) lean pork
15 ml (1 tbsp) Shaoxing rice wine	Salt and freshly ground black pepper
5 ml (1 tsp) sugar	1 carrot
2.5-cm (1-inch) piece root ginger, peeled and finely chopped	1 stick celery
	½ fennel bulb

Method

1

To make the sauce, in a small serving dish mix together the soy sauce, wine, sugar and ginger.
Allow to stand for 30 minutes for the flavours to develop before serving.

2

Meanwhile, cut the pork into very thin slices and season with salt and pepper.

3

Cut the carrot, celery and fennel into thin julienne strips. Place in a Chinese bamboo steamer and steam
over a large pan or wok of boiling water for 3 minutes.

4

Remove the steamer from the pan and lay the slices of pork over the vegetables. Return the steamer to the pan
or wok and steam for a further 5 minutes.

5

Serve the pork and vegetables accompanied by the cold sauce.

Serving suggestion

Serve on individual plates garnished with fresh herb sprigs with small pools of the sauce
arranged around the pork and vegetables.

Variation

Use your own choice of vegetables for this dish.

Cook's tip

Cut the carrots into thinner strips than the celery, since they will take longer to cook.

Meat

Rice-Coated Meatballs

These highly seasoned meatballs, coated in rice, can be made with any minced meat of your choice.

Preparation time: 40 minutes, plus 2 hours soaking time • Cooking time: 15-20 minutes if you can
steam the meatballs in 1 batch, longer if you do 2 batches • Serves: 4

Ingredients

600 g (1 lb 5 oz) boned pork shoulder, minced	2.5 ml (¹/₂ tsp) soy sauce
2.5-cm (1-inch) piece root ginger, peeled and chopped	¹/₂ egg, beaten
	A dash of chilli sauce
2.5 ml (¹/₂ tsp) finely chopped shallots	Salt and freshly ground black pepper
2.5 ml (¹/₂ tsp) finely chopped fresh parsley	100 g (3¹/₂ oz) long-grain rice, pre-soaked in warm water for 2 hours and drained
2.5 ml (¹/₂ tsp) finely chopped fresh chives	

Method

1
In a bowl, mix together the pork, ginger, shallots, parsley, chives, soy sauce, egg and chilli sauce.
Stir well to combine all the ingredients thoroughly.

2
Season with salt and pepper, then form into small meatballs.

3
Drain the rice thoroughly in a fine sieve, shaking well to remove all the water. Spread the rice onto a clean work surface.

4
Roll the meatballs in the rice to coat them evenly.

5
Steam the meatballs for about 15 minutes in a Chinese bamboo steamer over a large pan or wok of boiling water.
The exact cooking time will depend on the thickness of the meatballs.

Serving suggestion
Serve with Vegetable Chop Suey (see page 78 for recipe).

Variation
Try beef, veal or chicken in place of the pork.

Cook's tip
Rinse your hands in cold water before shaping the meatballs, otherwise they tend to stick to the bamboo steamer and break up.

Beef with Ginger Sauce

Quick-fried beef with fresh root ginger, served in a soy and tomato sauce.

Preparation time: 15 minutes • Cooking time: 5 minutes • Serves: 4

Ingredients

450 g (1 lb) fillet of beef	*5 ml (1 tsp) sugar*
30 ml (2 tbsp) oil	*15 ml (1 tbsp) red wine vinegar*
30 ml (2 tbsp) root ginger, peeled and cut into small matchsticks	*30 ml (2 tbsp) soy sauce*
2 tomatoes, peeled, seeded and finely chopped	*Salt and freshly ground pepper, to taste*

Method

1

Cut the beef into very thin slices.

2

Heat the oil in a wok, add the meat and the ginger and stir-fry for 1 minute.

3

Pour off any excess fat, then stir in the tomatoes. Reduce the heat and add the sugar, wine vinegar and soy sauce.

4

Cook for a few minutes to allow the flavours to develop, then season with salt and pepper and serve immediately.

Serving suggestion

Serve with tomatoes, lightly seasoned with salt and pepper and heated through in a Chinese bamboo steamer over a large pan or wok of boiling water.

Cook's tip

Avoid cooking the ginger too long, otherwise its fragrant flavour will be impaired.

Pork with Green Peppers

A quickly prepared stir-fried pork dish with green peppers and a hoisin-based sauce.

Preparation time: 15 minutes • Cooking time: 6-8 minutes • Serves: 4

Ingredients

450 g (1 lb) pork fillet	*5 ml (1 tsp) wine vinegar*
30 ml (2 tbsp) oil	*30 ml (2 tbsp) chicken stock*
2.5 ml (½ tsp) chopped garlic	*15 ml (1 tbsp) hoisin sauce*
2 green peppers, seeded and cut into thin matchsticks	*Salt and freshly ground black pepper, to taste*
	5 ml (1 tsp) cornflour, combined with a little water

Method

1

Thinly slice the pork, then cut into thin strips.

2

Heat the oil in a wok. Add the garlic, peppers and the pork. Stir together well.
Cook for 1 minute, shaking the wok occasionally.

3

Stir in the vinegar, stock and hoisin sauce. Season with salt and pepper. Cook for 3 minutes.

4

Stir in the cornflour paste and cook, stirring continuously, until the sauce has thickened. Serve immediately.

Serving suggestion

If you like a touch of chilli heat, as a foil to the sweetness of the sauce finely chop a seeded red chilli pepper
and sprinkle over the dish before serving.

Variation

Use red peppers in place of the green peppers.

Pork in Sweet-and-Sour Sauce

The sweet and sour flavours are perfectly balanced in this flavourful pork dish.

Preparation time: 25 minutes • Cooking time: 12-15 minutes • Serves: 4

Ingredients

1 onion	15 ml (1 tbsp) sugar
¼ cucumber	½ tomato, peeled, seeded and finely chopped
½ red pepper, seeded	300 ml (½ pint) chicken stock
½ green pepper, seeded	30 ml (2 tbsp) oil
1 slice pineapple, fresh or canned	450 g (1 lb) pork, cut into thin strips
60 ml (4 tbsp) pineapple juice	1 clove garlic, chopped
45 ml (3 tbsp) wine vinegar	5 ml (1 tsp) cornflour, combined with a little water
5 ml (1 tsp) chilli sauce	Salt and freshly ground black pepper, to taste

Method

1

Cut the onion, cucumber, red and green pepper and pineapple into thin matchsticks.

2

In a small bowl, mix together the pineapple juice, wine vinegar, chilli sauce, sugar, tomato and stock. Set aside.

3

Heat the oil in a wok, and stir-fry the pork and garlic. Once the meat is golden brown, remove with a slotted spoon and set aside.

4

Add all the vegetables and the pineapple to the wok and stir-fry for 2 minutes.

5

Return the pork to the wok with the vegetables and pineapple, and pour over the contents of the bowl.
Cook for 3-4 minutes, stirring and shaking the wok from time to time.

6

Add the cornflour paste gradually, stirring continuously until the sauce has thickened.
Season with salt and pepper. Serve piping hot.

Serving suggestion

Serve with Stir-Fried Sticky Rice (see page 86 for recipe).

Variation

Use orange juice in place of the pineapple juice.

Cook's tip

Stir-fry the vegetables quickly so that they remain slightly crisp.

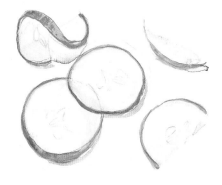

Chicken and Bean Sprout Salad

Steamed chicken and bean sprouts, coated in a refreshingly light sauce.

Preparation time: 20 minutes, plus 20 minutes standing time • Cooking time: 20 minutes • Serves: 4

Ingredients

400 g (14 oz) bean sprouts	5 ml (1 tsp) sugar
300 g (10½ oz) chicken breast	15 ml (1 tbsp) soy sauce
5 ml (1 tsp) soy sauce	A pinch of chopped garlic
	15 ml (1 tbsp) peanut oil
For the sauce	2.5 ml (½ tsp) sesame oil
30 ml (2 tbsp) chopped chives	Salt and freshly
15 ml (1 tbsp) white wine vinegar	ground black pepper

Method

1

To prepare the sauce, mix together all the ingredients in a small bowl, and season with a little salt and pepper.
Allow to stand for 20 minutes.

2

Meanwhile, cook the bean sprouts for 2 minutes in boiling water. Drain and refresh under cold water.
Set aside to drain completely.

3

Sprinkle the chicken with the soy sauce and steam in a Chinese bamboo steamer over
a large pan or wok of boiling water for about 15 minutes, until cooked through.

4

Remove the chicken from the steamer, set aside to cool, then thinly slice.

5

Mix together the bean sprouts and chicken. Pour over the sauce and serve.

Serving suggestion

For an attractive presentation for a dinner party, on a large serving platter, fan the slices of chicken in a circle
and heap the bean sprouts in the centre. Add whole fresh chives at intervals around the circle, then sprinkle the
whole dish with some finely chopped chives.

Variation

Instead of steaming, the chicken could be cooked in stock, to which the soy sauce has been added.

Cook's tip

Mix together the sauce ingredients the day before serving the dish, to allow the flavours more time to develop.

Bean Sprout Salad

This light and colourful salad can be served as a light lunch or a starter to any Chinese meal.

Preparation time: 20 minutes • Cooking time: 15 minutes • Serves: 4

Ingredients

400 g (14 oz) bean sprouts	30 ml (2 tbsp) soy sauce
½ red pepper, seeded	Salt and freshly ground black pepper
1 carrot	15 ml (1 tbsp) oil
½ cucumber	2.5 ml (½ tsp) sugar
2 slices ham	1 drop wine vinegar
2.5 ml (½ tsp) chopped garlic	15 ml (1 tbsp) peeled, seeded and finely chopped tomato
2.5 ml (½ tsp) chilli sauce	10 ml (2 tsp) sesame oil

Method

1

Cook the bean sprouts in boiling water for 15 minutes. Refresh in cold water and set aside to drain.

2

Meanwhile, cut the pepper, carrot, cucumber and ham into thin strips.

3

To make the dressing, in a bowl, mix together the chopped garlic, chilli sauce, soy sauce, salt and pepper, oil, sugar, wine vinegar and tomato. Stir together well.

4

In a large bowl, toss together the bean sprouts, vegetables and ham. Pour over the dressing and the sesame oil and toss again. Serve chilled.

Serving suggestion
Sprinkle with freshly chopped chives before serving.

Variation
The bean sprouts can be used raw if you prefer a crunchier texture.

Cook's tip
If fresh bean sprouts are not available, use the canned variety. Rinse under cold running water and use directly in the salad – there is no need to cook them.

Chinese Leaf and Cucumber Salad

Crisply cooked Chinese leaves marinated with cucumber in a slightly sweet sauce.

Preparation time: 20 minutes, plus 2 hours marinating time • Cooking time: 5 minutes • Serves: 4

Ingredients

400 g (14 oz) Chinese leaves, thinly sliced	30 ml (2 tbsp) sesame oil
1 clove garlic	400 g (14 oz) cucumber, thinly sliced
15 ml (1 tbsp) soy sauce	Salt and freshly ground black pepper, to taste
5 ml (1 tsp) sugar	

Method

1
Blanch the Chinese leaves in boiling, salted water for 1 minute. Set aside to drain.

2
Slice the garlic clove in half and remove the core. Crush each half with the blade of a knife and finely chop.

3
To make the marinade, in a small bowl, mix together the garlic, soy sauce, sugar and sesame oil.

4
In a serving bowl, mix together the Chinese leaves and cucumber, and season with salt and pepper.

5
Pour over the marinade and set aside at room temperature for 2 hours. Serve at room temperature.

Serving suggestion
Garnish with sprigs of fresh herbs before serving.

Variation
Use a light or mushroom-flavoured soy sauce in place of the ordinary soy sauce.

Vegetable Stir-Fry

A delicious combination of Chinese vegetables and nuts, stir-fried in a little oil, then cooked in an aromatic sauce.

Preparation time: 25 minutes, plus soaking time • Cooking time: 55 minutes • Serves: 4

Ingredients

2 dried lotus roots, soaked overnight in water	115 g (4 oz) dried Chinese black mushrooms, soaked for 1 hour in warm water and drained
30 ml (2 tbsp) oil	1 courgette, thinly sliced
150 g (5½ oz) bean sprouts	100 g (3½ oz) frozen peas
½ red pepper, seeded and finely chopped	30 ml (2 tbsp) cashew nuts, roughly chopped
½ green pepper, seeded and finely chopped	5 ml (1 tsp) sugar
½ spring onion, chopped	30 ml (2 tbsp) soy sauce
300 g (10½ oz) Chinese leaves, finely chopped	400 ml (14 fl oz) chicken stock
	Salt and freshly ground black pepper

Method

1
Cook the lotus roots in boiling, lightly salted water for 20 minutes. Thinly slice.

2
Heat the oil in a wok and stir-fry each of the following ingredients separately, in order, for 30 seconds each, removing the first ingredient before adding the next: bean sprouts, peppers, spring onion, Chinese leaves, lotus root, mushrooms, courgette, peas and cashew nuts.

3
Return all the ingredients to the wok and stir in the sugar, soy sauce and stock.

4
Season with salt and pepper and cook for 30 minutes, stirring frequently.

5
Serve the vegetables slightly drained of the sauce.

Serving suggestion
Serve as a main meal with boiled or steamed rice. Alternatively, serve as a special-occasion vegetable side dish.

Variation
Use walnuts, hazelnuts or almonds in place of the cashew nuts.

Vegetable Chop Suey

Stir-fried vegetables, simmered in a wok with chicken stock and soy sauce.

Preparation time: 25 minutes • Cooking time: 6-8 minutes • Serves: 4

Ingredients

1 green pepper, seeded	*2 cloves garlic*
1 red pepper, seeded	*30 ml (2 tbsp) oil*
1 carrot	*10 ml (2 tsp) sugar*
½ cucumber	*30 ml (2 tbsp) soy sauce*
1 courgette, thickly peeled and the central core discarded	*100 ml (3½ fl oz) chicken stock*
1 onion	*Salt and freshly ground black pepper, to taste*

Method

1
Cut all the vegetables into thin slices. Slice the onion in half, then into quarters and finally into thin, even slices. Chop the garlic very finely.

2
Heat the oil in a wok and stir-fry the peppers and garlic for 30 seconds.

4
Add the onion and the carrot, and stir-fry for a further 30 seconds.

5
Add the cucumber and courgette, and cook for a further minute, stirring and shaking the wok continuously.

6
Stir in the sugar, soy sauce, stock and salt and pepper, mixing the ingredients together thoroughly. Simmer for about 3 minutes, until all the ingredients are fully incorporated. Serve immediately.

Serving suggestion
Serve as a main meal with boiled Chinese egg noodles, or serve as a side dish with a stir-fried pork or chicken dish.

Variation
Add blanched bean sprouts or sliced, blanched bamboo shoots and stir-fry with the cucumber and courgette, if you like.

Fried Noodles with Pork and Vegetables

The noodles in this dish are deep-fried to make them appetisingly crisp.

Preparation time: 20 minutes • Cooking time: 25 minutes • Serves: 4

Ingredients

350 g (12 oz) fresh egg noodles	*225 g (8 oz) cooked pork meat, thinly sliced*
1 taro	*15 ml (1 tbsp) soy sauce*
15 ml (1 tbsp) oil	*300 ml (½ pint) chicken stock*
5 ml (1 tsp) chopped garlic	*Salt and freshly ground black pepper*
1 carrot, cut into sticks	*Oil for deep-frying*
225 g (8 oz) Chinese leaves, thinly sliced	*5 ml (1 tsp) cornflour, combined with a little water*

Method

1
Cook the noodles in boiling, salted water for about 3 minutes, until just tender. Rinse in warm water and set aside to drain.
Slice off the end of the taro, then peel with a potato peeler. Using the peeler, cut the taro into thin slices.

2
Heat the oil in a wok and stir-fry the taro, garlic, carrot and Chinese leaves for about 1 minute.

3
Add the pork, soy sauce, stock and salt and pepper. Cook over a gentle heat for 5 minutes, shaking the wok frequently.

4
Heat the oil in a deep saucepan or deep-fryer to 180°C/350°F and fry the noodles a few at a time until crisp and golden.
Drain on absorbent kitchen paper.

5
Share the noodles equally between 4 small serving plates.

6
Strain the vegetable and pork mixture from the wok and spoon over the noodles. Keep warm.

7
Add the cornflour paste to the remaining sauce in the wok, stirring continuously until the sauce thickens.
Pour some of the sauce over each plate and serve immediately.

Serving suggestion
Garnish with fresh herb sprigs and chopped fresh chives before serving.

Cook's tips
To keep the noodles warm and crisp while you thicken the sauce, place in a warm oven. Make sure the noodles
are completely dry before cooking them in the oil, to avoid spattering.

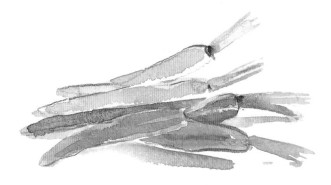

Noodles with Ginger and Oyster Sauce

Noodles stir-fried with ginger, carrot and courgette, then served in an oyster sauce.

Preparation time: 20 minutes • Cooking time: 10 minutes • Serves: 4

Ingredients

225 g (8 oz) Chinese dried egg or wheat noodles	1 spring onion, cut into thin rounds
1 carrot	15 ml (1 tbsp) oil
1 courgette	15 ml (1 tbsp) soy sauce
3 slices root ginger	30 ml (2 tbsp) oyster sauce
	Salt and freshly ground black pepper

Method

1

Cook the noodles in boiling, salted water for about 4-5 minutes, until just tender. Rinse under cold water and set aside to drain.

2

Cut the carrot into thin strips. Thickly peel the courgette to include a little of the flesh and cut into thin strips. Discard the core of the courgette.

3

Peel the ginger sparingly, removing any hard parts. Using a potato peeler, cut into thin slices, then cut the slices into thin strips using a very sharp knife. Heat the oil in a wok and stir-fry the spring onion for 10 seconds. Add the carrot, courgette and ginger, and stir-fry for 30 seconds.

4

Stir in the noodles and stir-fry for 1 minute.

5

Stir in the soy and oyster sauces and continue cooking until heated through. Season with salt and pepper. Serve immediately.

Serving suggestion

Serve as an accompaniment to stir-fried pork or chicken dishes.

Variation

Cook the noodles in chicken stock for extra flavour.

Cook's tip

Stir-fry the ginger and vegetables quickly to avoid browning.

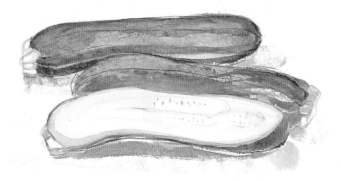

Seafood Chow Mein

Chinese egg noodles cooked with mussels, cockles and vegetables, served in a rich ginger and wine flavoured sauce.

Preparation time: 20 minutes • Cooking time: 12-15 minutes • Serves: 4

Ingredients

225 g (8 oz) Chinese dried egg or wheat noodles	½ spring onion, chopped
½ green pepper, seeded	150 g (5½ oz) uncooked shelled mussels
½ red pepper, seeded	50 g (1¾ oz) uncooked shelled cockles
15 ml (1 tbsp) oil	15 ml (1 tbsp) Shaoxing rice wine
2.5 ml (½ tsp) chopped garlic	30 ml (2 tbsp) soy sauce
2.5 ml (½ tsp) chopped root ginger	Salt and freshly ground black pepper, to taste

Method

1

Cook the noodles in boiling, salted water for about 4-5 minutes, until just tender. Rinse under cold water and set aside to drain.

2

Meanwhile, cut the peppers into thin slices.

3

Heat the oil in a wok and stir-fry the garlic, ginger, peppers and spring onion for 1 minute.

4

Stir in the mussels, cockles, wine, soy sauce and the cooked noodles.

5

Using chopsticks, mix together well. Season with salt and pepper, and cook for about 5 minutes, stirring frequently, until the seafood is cooked through. Serve immediately.

Serving suggestion

Serve this sumptuous dish as a special-occasion fish course.

Variation

Use a selection of seafood of your own choice.

Stir-Fried Sticky Rice

A flavoursome rice dish combining glutinous rice with stir-fried mushrooms, ginger and shallots.

Preparation time: 20 minutes, plus 8 hours soaking time • Cooking time: 25 minutes • Serves: 4

Ingredients

250 g (9 oz) glutinous rice, soaked for 8 hours	1 slice root ginger
30 ml (2 tbsp) oil	4 dried Chinese black mushrooms, soaked for 15 minutes in warm water, drained and sliced
2 spring onions, chopped	
½ onion, chopped	Salt and freshly ground black pepper, to taste

Method

1

Wash the rice in plenty of cold water and place in a sieve. Pour 1.3 litres (2¼ pints) boiling water over the rice and set aside.

2

Heat the oil in a wok and stir-fry the onions and ginger for about 2-3 minutes, until golden brown.

3

Add the mushrooms and stir-fry for about 1 minute.

4

Add the rice and enough of the water to cover the rice by 1.25 cm (½ inch). Stir well.

5

Cover and cook over a moderate heat until there is almost no liquid left. Reduce the heat and continue cooking until all the liquid has been absorbed. This process takes about 20 minutes in total.

6

Add salt and pepper. Remove the ginger and serve immediately.

Serving suggestion
Sprinkle over some chopped fresh chives before serving.

Variation
Replace the water with beef stock for extra flavour.

Stir-Fried Rice with Peppers

Long-grain rice stir-fried with red and green peppers, onions and soy sauce.

Preparation time: 10 minutes • Cooking time: 15-20 minutes • Serves: 4

Ingredients

100 g (3½ oz) long-grain rice	1 red pepper, seeded and cut into very thin strips
15 ml (1 tbsp) peanut oil	15 ml (1 tbsp) soy sauce
1 onion, chopped	Salt and freshly ground black pepper
1 green pepper, seeded and cut into very thin strips	5 ml (1 tsp) sesame oil

Method

1

Cook the rice in boiling water for about 10-12 minutes, until just tender. Drain and set aside.

2

Heat the oil in a wok and stir-fry the onion for about 1 minute. Add the peppers and continue to stir-fry for a further minute, until lightly browned.

3

Add the rice to the wok, stir in the soy sauce and continue cooking until the rice is heated through completely.

4

Season with salt, pepper and the sesame oil and serve.

Serving suggestion

Serve as a colourful and flavourful accompaniment to any Chinese meat, poultry or game dish.

Variation

Use sesame oil for stir-frying the vegetables in place of peanut oil.

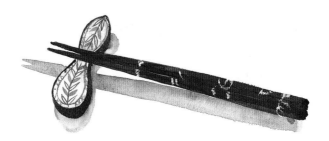

Melon Salad

A refreshing fruit salad, ideal for serving after a rich meal of many courses.

Preparation time: 30 minutes, plus 3 hours or more chilling time • Serves: 4

Ingredients

1 large cantaloupe melon	*4 large or 8 small fresh strawberries*
1 mango	*4 canned lychees, plus reserved juice from the can*

Method

1
Peel and seed the melon, then cut into thin slices.

2
Peel and stone the mango, then cut into thin slices.

3
Using a melon baller, cut as many balls as possible from the strawberries.

4
Arrange the melon slices evenly on 4 small serving plates.

5
Spread a layer of mango over the melon. Place a lychee in the centre of each plate and arrange a few strawberry balls around the lychee.

6
Divide the lychee juice evenly between the plates. Chill in the refrigerator before serving.

Serving suggestion
Serve with a scoop of melon or strawberry sorbet or, for a richer dessert, vanilla ice-cream.

Variations
Use small whole raspberries in place of the strawberry balls. Use papaya in place of the mango.

Cook's tip
This dessert is best served after several hours of chilling.

Exotic Fruit Salad

Fresh fruit marinated in orange and lychee juice with just a hint of almond.

Preparation time: 1 hour, plus 3 hours or more marinating time • Serves: 4

Ingredients

1 fully ripe papaya	*3 blood oranges*
1 pomegranate	*4 canned lychees, plus reserved juice from the can*
4 rambutan fruit	*3 drops bitter almond essence or ordinary almond essence*
2 kiwi fruit	

Method

1

To prepare the papaya, cut in half and, using a small spoon, scoop out the pips and any stringy flesh. Discard. Peel each half and cut the flesh into thin slices. Place in a bowl.

2

To prepare the pomegranate, cut in half and scoop out the pulp and seeds. Discard the remainder of the fruit. Cut the pulp into cubes and add the pulp and seeds to the bowl with the papaya.

3

To prepare the rambutan, holding the fruit over the bowl, cut through the skin with a knife, then peel the fruit. Cut the flesh into slices and add to the bowl with the other fruit.

4

Peel, then slice the kiwi fruit and add to the bowl.

5

Peel two of the oranges. Remove all the pith and cut the flesh into small pieces. Add to the bowl. Add the lychees and carefully stir the contents of the bowl.

6

Squeeze the juice from the remaining orange into a small bowl. Add the lychee juice and almond essence, and stir well.

7

Pour the juice and almond essence mixture over the fruit and leave the salad to marinate for several hours in the refrigerator.

8

Serve chilled.

Serving suggestion

Garnish the fruit salad with sprigs of fresh mint just before serving.

Variation

Use mango or melon in place of the papaya.

Kumquats with Crystallised Ginger

This dessert will delight anyone with a sweet tooth!

Preparation time: 20 minutes, plus cooling and chilling time • Cooking time: 1 hour 50 minutes • Serves: 4

Ingredients

20 kumquats	*225 g (8 oz) sugar*
2.5-cm (1-inch) piece root ginger, peeled and sliced	

Method

1
Wash the kumquats thoroughly. Blanch in boiling water and drain.

2
Blanch the ginger in boiling water and drain.

3
Place the kumquats in a saucepan with the sugar. Cover with water to a level of 5 cm (2 inches) above the fruit.
Add the ginger and bring to the boil.

4
Reduce the heat and allow the liquid to reduce and caramelise gently. This process will take about 1½ hours.
Add a little more water during cooking, if necessary.

5
Allow the dish to cool, then chill in the refrigerator.

6
Remove the ginger, cut into very small pieces, then return to the dish. Serve.

Serving suggestions

Cut the ginger into small diamond shapes and arrange in a pattern on individual serving plates around the kumquats.
Cut a few fresh mint leaves into very thin strips and sprinkle over the kumquats before serving.

Cook's tip

Cook the kumquats and ginger very slowly, so that the sugar penetrates to the centre of the fruit.

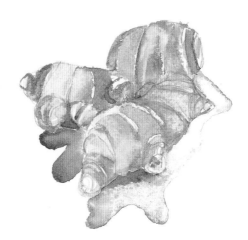

Index